Were dinosaurs smart ?

Disney BOOKS BY MAIL

DK Direct Limited
Managing Art Editor Eljay Crompton
Senior Editor Rosemary McCormick
Writer Alexandra Parsons
Illustrators The Alvin White Studios and Richard Manning
Designers Amanda Barlow, Wayne Blades, Veneta Bullen,
Richard Clemson, Sarah Goodwin, Diane Klein, Sonia Whillock

Contents

What did the world look like when dinosaurs were alive?

The weather was warm and rainy. There were trees with spiny leaves, and lots of ferns and shrubs that grew close to the ground. There were ponds, lakes, and forests, but no towns, houses, or roads, and – no people!

4

Time travelers

Even though there were no people around when dinosaurs were alive, let's pretend we're climbing into a time machine and zooming back millions of years to see their world!

A long time!
Dinosaurs
lived on Earth
for nearly 150 million
years. Different dinosaurs lived
at different times in history. The
first dinosaurs appeared around
200 million years ago.

Land and sea
The world looked different
then. All the land was in one
great lump with the sea all
around it. But little by little, over
millions of years, the land broke
up into pieces we call continents.

Where did baby dinosaurs come from?

They hatched out of eggs. Mother dinosaurs laid their eggs in nests on the ground. They lined their nests with leaves and ferns. Some baby dinosaurs were tiny but strong, and they could walk as soon as they had pecked their way out of their eggs.

Pitter patter

Scientists have found baby dino footprints left in mud – which over millions of years turned to rock. Because of these footprints, we know that adult dinosaurs marched on the outside of the herd, while the baby dinos raced around safely in the middle.

Who says?

How do we know about dinosaur nests? Because some nests got buried beneath layers and layers of mud. The nests were protected by the mud for millions of years until people discovered them.

Dino egg facts

☞ The biggest dinosaur egg ever found was the size of a football.

☞ There were egg-eating dinosaurs that stole eggs from other dino nests.

Were dinosaurs smart?

They were about as smart as many animals that live in our world today. Scientists have figured out that the big dinos were about as smart as snakes, lizards, and toads. And some of the smaller ones may have been as clever as birds – which is kind of medium-smart, for an animal.

Smarty-pants

This dinosaur is thought to have been the smartest of all. It's called *Troodon* (TRUE-oh-don). For its size, it had a big brain and big eyes.

Brainy facts

☞ A lot of dinos had big heads, but not much brain inside. Most of the space was taken up with muscle and bone instead.

☞ The skull of *Allosaurus* (AL-oh-saw-rus) had great big holes in it so it wouldn't be too heavy.

2 + 2 = 4

3 + 3

9 8

Zzzzzzzzz!
Did you hear about the *Stegosaurus*
who bought a sleeping bag?
**He spent two months trying to
wake it up!**

The dunce
This *Stegosaurus*
(STEG-oh-SAW-rus) is
probably the dumbest dino
there was. It weighed as
much as an elephant,
and had a brain the
size of a walnut.

How do we know what dinosaurs looked like?

Because the dinosaurs left a lot of clues behind. They left their bones and teeth. They also left their footprints, imprints of their whole bodies, and even nests full of eggs. These remains are called fossils. They are images that have been kept safe in rocks, stone, sand, and mud.

Careful now!

Digging up a fossil is very tricky. Each piece of bone is wrapped up in special bandages before it is lifted out of the ground.

Jigsaw puzzle

This is a very old drawing of an *Iguanodon* (i-GWAN-na-DON). An *Iguanodon* tooth was the first fossil ever found.

Dino discovery facts

 From looking at bones, scientists can figure out the shape of the dinosaur's body.

There were over 800 different kinds of dinosaurs.

Are there any dinosaurs alive today?

No. The last ones died millions of years ago. Of course, there are still plenty of lizards around that look a little like dinosaurs. But it may come as a surprise to learn that the creatures most closely related to the dinosaurs are alligators and – birds!

Four claws
These birds are hoatzins and they come from South America. When they are young they have claws on their wings and their feet – similar to *Archaeopteryx* (ARK-ee-OP-ter-icks), an unusual bird that lived millions of years ago!

Bird power
Birds have been flying around on Earth for 150 million years.

Who was there?

☞ Crocodiles and alligators have been snapping in rivers since the time of the dinosaurs, and they still look very much the way they did back then.

☞ There's a spiny lizard-like animal called the tuatara – found only on the islands off New Zealand – that's a relative of a lizard that lived at the same time as the dinosaurs.

13

How fast could dinosaurs run?

We don't know for sure because there was no one around to time them. But dinosaur experts think that the smaller dinosaurs with big back legs and small heads, such as *Gallimimus* (GAL-im-EE-mus), could zip along at nearly 30 mph. *Gallimimus* sure looks like he's winning this race!

Odd bird
The ostrich is a very fast moving bird. You can see how alike the ostrich and *Gallimimus* look. Dino experts think that many of the speedier little dinosaurs looked a lot like ostriches.

14

Shadow surprise
What's as big as a dinosaur
and weighs nothing?
Its shadow!

Who's last?
The biggest dinosaurs were the
slowest movers. This is *Diplodocus*
(dip-PLOD-uh-cuss). You can just
see its head here, but the end of its
tail is 86 feet away, or the length
of a subway train.

Fast-moving facts

 All the fast-movers had long back legs
and short front legs.

The speedy dinos were slender but
strong, and they had very powerful
muscles, strong ankles, and
narrow feet.

Could dinosaurs fly?

Dinosaurs couldn't fly, but one of their neighbors tried very hard. *Archaeopteryx*, or Archy to its friends, was an unusual kind of bird. It had a feathered body, wings with clawed fingers on them, and claws for feet. Archy probably ran around chasing insects and flapping its wings.

Important find

We know a lot about Archy because of this well preserved fossil. It was found in Germany over 100 years ago. You can see its head, wing feathers, and bones.

Flap and fly!
Some reptiles from dino times could fly. This flying reptile is called a pterosaur (TER-uh-SOR).

Creature facts

 There were other reptiles in the world long before dinosaurs.

Dinosaurs were reptiles, but they were different from the reptiles of today. Their legs did not stick out to the side like lizards' do. Instead, they walked around with their legs held underneath them.

How did dinosaurs keep cool?

Dino experts, who are called paleontologists, (PAL-ee-on-TOL-oh-jists) think that they did different things to stay cool and warm. *Stegosaurus* had huge, bony plates on its back which acted like a heating and cooling system. Blood flowed through the plates and was either cooled by breezes or warmed by the sun.

Cool dinos

Other dinosaurs may have looked for a nice shady place to stand when they felt uncomfortably hot.

Weird and wonderful dino facts

☞ Dinosaur means "terrible lizard" in Greek.

☞ The smallest dino was *Compsognathus* (COMP-sog-NAY-thus), which was the size of a chicken and had a very long tail. It ran after insects.

☞ *Hadrosaurs* (HAD- row-sor) had bony crests on their heads that probably made their voices sound louder.

Phewwwww!
What do you get if you cross a dinosaur with a skunk?
A big stink!

What did dinosaurs eat for lunch?

Some dinosaurs ate plants, and some of them ate other dinosaurs! The meat-eaters had sharp, pointed teeth for tearing their food. The plant-eaters had big, blunt teeth for grinding leaves and twigs. There was plenty of food for all of them.

Spiky snack
Over millions of years some plants grew spikier because they were tired of being eaten. Smaller dinosaurs got tired of being eaten, too, and over time they developed thick, scaly skin and sharp, pointy spikes.

Munch time

☞ Plants and dinos getting spiky didn't stop dinos from eating them. As plants and little dinos got spikier and spikier, dino jaws and teeth got stronger. Their stomachs also changed so they could swallow tough scales and prickly spikes. But these changes didn't happen suddenly, they happened over MILLIONS of years.

Were all dinosaurs fierce and frightening?

Some were. They were the dinosaurs that ate meat. Dinosaurs that ate meat had to fight other dinosaurs – usually the ones that just ate plants – and so looking scary and having large, pointy teeth was very helpful.

What a heavyweight!
One of the biggest and heaviest dinosaurs was *Brachiosaurus* (BRACK-ee-o-SAW-rus). It weighed more than 3,000 boys and girls put together. A dino that size would certainly frighten its enemies!

Mighty dino
This dino is
a *Tyrannosaurus*
(tie-RAN-oh-SAW-rus).
It is thought to have been the
largest and fiercest hunter in the
dinosaur world.

Dynamic dino facts

Nobody knows what color dinosaurs
were. They could have been blue, or
pink with purple spots, but probably
they were a greenish-brown to blend
in with their background.

And the winner is.......!
What happens when dinosaurs hold
beauty contests?
Nobody wins!

Why did some dinosaurs have big tails?

To whack their enemies in the knees during a fight. *Ankylosaurus* (an-KILE-o-SAW-rus), for instance, had a heavy, bony club at the end of its tail. *Stegosaurus's* tail had sharp spikes, and *Sauropod's* (SAW-row-pod) tail acted like a whip. Ouch!

Take that!

Ankylosaurus was much shorter than huge *Tyrannosaurus*, but with a well-aimed blow, little Anky could knock *Tyrannosaurus* to the ground.

Balancing tail

Ornithomimus (OR-nith-oh-MEE-mus) was a dino that used its tail to keep its balance as it ran around.

A tail for sitting on

Diplodocus used its tail to lean on. This way, it could stand tall on its back legs and frighten off its enemies.

Tail ends

Dinos that used their tails to whack their enemies had four feet and ate plants.

Dinos that used their tails for balance had two feet and two tiny arms, and they were often meat-eaters.

Why did dinosaurs disappear?

Nobody really knows the answer to that one, although there are many different ideas. Some people think they got a disease and died. Other people think that the dinos were killed when a big rock from outer space hit the earth, causing earthquakes and tidal waves. And other people think that the world just got too cold for them. But at least we do know they were here.

26

What came next?

☞ After the dinosaurs, the world slowly got colder and colder, and eventually it entered a time called the Ice Age. During the Ice Age, giant wooly mammoths, bison, and bears roamed around the earth.

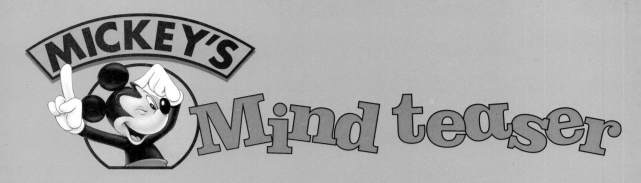

MICKEY'S Mind teaser

Each type of dinosaur behaved a certain way. Answer these questions to see how much you remember about them.

1. Was Tyrannosaurus large and fierce?

2. What did Archaeopteryx try hard to do?

3. Was Gallimimus a slow or fast mover?

4. Where did baby dinos come from?